Teachers

Quinn M. Arnold

CREATIVE EDUCATION • CREATIVE PAPERBACKS

seedlings

j 371.1 ARN

Published by Creative Education and Creative Paperbacks
P.O. Box 227, Mankato, Minnesota 56002
Creative Education and Creative Paperbacks
are imprints of The Creative Company
www.thecreativecompany.us

Design by Ellen Huber; production by Christine Vanderbeek
Art direction by Rita Marshall
Printed in the United States of America

Photographs by Alamy (Michael Dwyer, Lynnette Peizer), iStockphoto (asiseeit, IPGGutenbergUKLtd, monkeybusinessimages, percds), Shutterstock (AlexeiLogvinovich, antoniodiaz, Emil Durov, ESB Professional, littleny, Maglara, Jordi Muray, Picsfive, Olga Popova, SpeedKingz, Alex Staroseltsev, wavebreakmedia)

Copyright © 2018 Creative Education, Creative Paperbacks
International copyright reserved in all countries. No part of this book may be reproduced in any form without written permission from the publisher.

Library of Congress Cataloging-in-Publication Data
Names: Arnold, Quinn M., author.
Title: Teachers / Quinn M. Arnold.
Series: Seedlings.
Includes bibliographical references and index.
Summary: A kindergarten-level introduction to teachers, covering their job description, the places where they work, and how they help the community by using their instructional skills.
Identifiers: LCCN 2016059800
ISBN 978-1-60818-875-8 (hardcover)
ISBN 978-1-62832-490-7 (pbk)
ISBN 978-1-56660-923-4 (eBook)
Subjects: LCSH: Teachers—Juvenile literature.
Classification: LCC LB1775.A72 2017 / DDC 371.1—dc23
CCSS: RI.K.1, 2, 3, 4, 5, 6, 7;
RI.1.1, 2, 3, 4, 5, 6, 7; RF.K.1, 3; RF.1.1

First Edition HC 9 8 7 6 5 4 3 2 1
First Edition PBK 9 8 7 6 5 4 3 2 1

TABLE OF CONTENTS

Hello, Teachers! 4

Community Educators 7

Classroom Cooperation 8

Homework and Tests 10

Report Cards 12

In a School 15

What Do Teachers Do? 16

Goodbye, Teachers! 18

Picture a Teacher 20

Words to Know 22

Read More 23

Websites 23

Index 24

Hello, teachers!

Teachers explain many **subjects**. They show how to do math and science.

They teach reading and writing.

Most teachers work in schools.

Some work in homes.

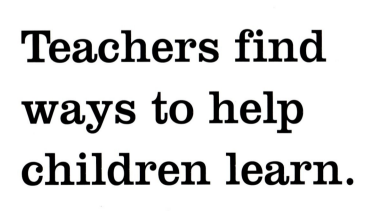

Teachers find ways to help children learn.

Teachers give homework and tests. These help them track how students learn.

Teachers fill out report cards. Parents meet with teachers.

They talk about how their children are doing in class.

Teachers answer questions. They plan for class. They grade papers. They help kids set goals.

Teachers help students learn new things. They educate children in their community.

Goodbye, teachers!

Words to Know

goals: things to be done or accomplished

subjects: topics studied in school, like math, science, or history

Read More

Kidde, Rita. *What Do Teachers Do?*
New York: PowerKids Press, 2015.

Meister, Cari. *Teachers.*
Minneapolis: Jump!, 2014.

Websites

KidsHealth: What Makes a Great Teacher
http://kidshealth.org/en/kids/great-teacher.html?WT.ac=ctg
Find out what makes a good teacher—according to kids!

Super Coloring: Professions Coloring Pages
http://www.supercoloring.com/coloring-pages/people/professions
Find pictures of teachers, and print them out to color.

Note: Every effort has been made to ensure that the websites listed above are suitable for children, that they have educational value, and that they contain no inappropriate material. However, because of the nature of the Internet, it is impossible to guarantee that these sites will remain active indefinitely or that their contents will not be altered.

Index

classes 13, 15
homework 10
parents 12, 13
report cards 12
schools 8
students 9, 10, 16
subjects 7
tests 10